Secure management system for web

Ghada Salim Mohammed

Secure management system for website of E-library in a university

Secure management system for web site of Electronic library in an university and the role of it in E- learning

LAP LAMBERT Academic Publishing

Publisher:
LAP LAMBERT Academic Publishing
is a trademark of
International Book Market Service Ltd., member of OmniScriptum Publishing Group
17 Meldrum Street, Beau Bassin 71504, Mauritius

Printed at: see last page
ISBN: 978-620-0-47149-9

Secure management system for web site of Electronic library in an university and the role of it in E- learning

Ghada Salim Mohammed

gha_2090@yahoo.com

Abstract

In today's the digital libraries are being created for diverse communities and in the different fields , in which large numbers of users are distributed geographically can access the contents of large and diverse repositories of electronic objects such as ,images ,audio and video. Storage and copying of information are done either by downloading or by printing from a master file. In this work MySQL database and php is used to design the web site of special university and as a part of this web site is electronic library that specified for the students of this university only.

This work is designed by using various programming languages such HTML, CSS for the design of E-library Graphical User Interfaces (GUI), PHP as a server side scripting language and MySQL Database a Relational Database Management system (RDMS) to build the database of the designed E-library System. The designed E-library allows the administrator to edit, add and manage borrow and return of documents. The designed E-library can be accessed via internet from anywhere at any time via internet through web browser.

Table of Content

Chapter One: Introduction to E-Library

Chapter Two: Web Design Concepts

Chapter Three: Design and implementation

Chapter Four: Conclusions

List of Abbreviations

PHP	Hypertext Preprocessor
HTML	Hypertext Markup Language
XML	Extensible Markup Language
DHTML	Dynamic Hypertext Markup Language
CSS	Cascade Style Sheet
SQL	Query Structured Language
PDA	personal digital assistant
PC	Personal Computer

HTTP	Hyper Text Transfer Protocol
JSP	JavaScript Programming
TCP/IP	Transmit Control Protocol / Internet Protocol
WWW	World Wide Web
CERN	the European Laboratory for Particle Physics
URL	Universal Resource Locator

Introduction

1.1 Introduction

A **website** is a collection of related web pages, including multimedia content, typically identified with a common domain name, and published on at least one web server. A website may be accessible via a public Internet Protocol (IP) network by referencing a uniform resource locator (URL) that identifies it.

Web pages, which are the building blocks of websites, are documents, typically composed in plain text interspersed with formatting instructions of Hypertext Markup Language (HTML, XHTML). They may incorporate elements from other websites with suitable markup anchors. Web pages are accessed and transported with the Hypertext Transfer Protocol (HTTP), which may optionally employ encryption (HTTP Secure, HTTPS) to provide security and privacy for the user [1] .

Hyper linking between web pages conveys to the reader the site structure and guides the navigation of the site, which often starts with a home page containing a directory of the site web content. Some websites require user registration or subscription to access content.

A static website is one that has web pages stored on the server in the format that is sent to a client web browser. It is primarily coded in Hypertext Markup Language (HTML). Cascading Style Sheets (CSS) are used to control appearance beyond basic HTML[2]. Images are commonly used to effect the desired appearance and as part of the main content. Audio or video might also be considered "static" content if it plays automatically or is generally non-interactive. This type of website

1

usually displays the same information to all visitors. a static website will generally provide consistent, standard information for an extended period of time. Although the website owner may make updates periodically[3].

A dynamic website is one that changes or customizes itself frequently and automatically. Server-side dynamic pages are generated "on the fly" by computer code that produces the HTML (CSS are responsible for appearance and thus, are static files). There are a wide range of software systems, such as CGI, Java Servlets and Java Server Pages (JSP), Active Server Pages and ColdFusion (CFML) that are available to generate dynamic web systems and dynamic sites.[4]

1.2 Web Architecture

A typical web application involves four tiers as depicted in the following web architecture figure: web browsers on the client side for rendering data presentation coded in HTML, a web server program that generates data presentation, an application server program that computes business logic, and a database server program that provides data persistency. The three types of server programs may run on the same or different server machines[5].

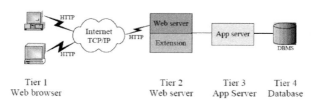

| Tier 1 | Tier 2 | Tier 3 | Tier 4 |
| Web browser | Web server | App Server | Database |

Web browsers can run on most operating systems with limited hardware or software requirement. They are the graphic user interface for the clients to interact with web applications. Apache, Tomcat and IIS are popular web server programs, and IE and Firefox are popular web browsers[5].

2

1.3 E-learning in Digital Libraries

Libraries were among pioneering institutions which introduced computer technology in their daily operations in the middle of 20th century and they continued to introduce new technological successes throughout the rest of the century to improve access to and use of library holdings. Major step forward in library development happened in the beginning of the 1990s when digital libraries were introduced. The concept of digital libraries was a major success from its very start as "it came out of closed walls of library and reached users in their home, workplace and even while traveling, with the help of laptops" [15].

Digital libraries "have emerged as a leading edge technological solution to the persistent problem of enhancing access, process of archiving and expanding the dissemination of information" [16]. Digital libraries generally speaking "consist of digital contents (which are sometimes but not necessarily text-based), interconnections (which may be simple links or complex metadata or query-based relationships), and software (which may be simple pages in HTML or complex database management systems)" [17]. More specifically, digital libraries offer "online catalogues, databases, multimedia, online journals, digital repositories, electronic books, electronic archives and online / electronic services" [18].

An electronic library is a heterogeneous system in which information is available in hard copy, on magnetic tape and discs, CD-ROMs and videodiscs, and also from online sources. Storage and copying of information are done either by downloading or by printing from a master file. Such libraries are can provide very diverse information; however, electronic libraries will evolve in an incremental fashion and, at least for the next few decades, we will operate in a dual paper-based and electronic environment. Digital library collections contain fixed permanent documents. While current libraries have more dynamic collections, a digital library

3

facilitates quicker handling of information. Digital libraries break the physical boundaries of data. Digital libraries are as important for communications and collaboration as for information seeking activities.

Most of our university libraries are now automated and many scholars have e-mail accounts. Communication and data transfer or interchange has become easy with the help of Internet and email attachments.

The concept of e-learning can be incorporated into a digital library system. For instance, in an e-learning environment the contents are truly dynamic. Any piece of information comes with a system that equips a user to test his level of knowledge. Libraries have adapted accordingly to enhance the learning process.

- **Preservation**

Libraries have preservation issues of all kinds to deal with, especially the deterioration of the paper collection. Digitizing as a means of preservation is quite beneficial. It helps to preserve rare and fragile objects without denying access to those who wish to study them. Convenience is also a benefit. Users can retrieve digitized books in seconds by searching for words, phrases or ideas. Several people can simultaneously read the same book or view the same picture. Another benefit is space. Electronic copies occupy millimeters of space rather than meters on shelf. Preservation concerns include deciding what to digitize, formats for texts and images, quality of images, and costs.

- **Technologies**

Digitization requires certain technologies. These include storage technologies—a variety of devices to store and retrieve information in digital form such as magnetic tapes/cassettes, floppy disks, hard disks, DAT Tape, CD-ROM, smart cards; processing technology—creating the systems and applications software that is required for the performance of digital network; communication technologies primarily to communicate information in digital form; display technologies varieties of output devices[13]

1.4 Digital library services for e-learning

Digital libraries are opened to the wide public and as such they offer many possibilities of inclusion of their content in formal and informal learning. Calhoun [14] investigated social roles of digital libraries which also include teaching, learning and the advancement of knowledge. For formal education, digital libraries can offer the following services: specialized educational digital libraries, portals for teachers or students, integration with learning management systems and access to primary sources [14].

For progress of knowledge digital libraries offer the following services: self-archiving, deposit incentives; mandatory deposit, open access journals. libraries as publishers, digital libraries of theses and dissertations, cross-repository services. object reuse and exchange services, workflow-based content creation and management. data curation and researcher profiling services [14], digital information resources usable on different electronic devices, library services for information discovery, course materials, exhibits, workshops etc.

Wangila [15] pointed out that "the integration of the digital library technology with the educational enterprise has come at a similar time when the student requirements for access to library resources also heightened". The same author suggests the need for policies, guidelines and standards to ensure professional efficiency and quality of information service delivery in digital library. In spite of wealth of materials and services, all digital libraries are not equal. Their differences define their possible use.

This part of the paper will present digital libraries which offer support for the learning process. The focus will be on the most famous world digital libraries as there is no one global register which would list all existing digital libraries offering educational resources. Since each digital library (and institution behind digital library) has its own approach to presenting learning and teaching materials, it is rather difficult to compare them against a fixed set of criteria

1.5 Benefits of Digital Libraries

Digital libraries bring significant benefits to the users through the following features [3]:

i. Improved access

Digital libraries are typically accessed through the Internet and Compact Disc-Read Only Memory (CD-ROM). They can be accessed virtually. from anywhere and at any time. They are not tied to the physical location and operating hours of traditional library.

ii. Wider access

A digital library can meet simultaneous access requests for a document by easily creating multiple instances or copies of the requested document. It can also meet the requirements of a larger population of users easily.

iii. Improved information sharing.

Through the appropriate metadata and information exchange protocols, the digital libraries can easily share information with other similar digital libraries and provide enhanced access to users.

iv. Improved preservation.

Since the electronic documents are not prone to physical wear and tear, their exact copies can easily be made, the digital libraries facilitate preservation of special and rare documents and artifacts by providing access to digital versions of these entities.

1.6   Functional Components of Digital Library

Most digital libraries share common functional components. These include [6]:

ii. Organization

The key process involved in this component is the assignment of the metadata (bibliographic information) to each document being added to the collection.

i. Selection and acquisition

The typical processes covered in this component include the selection of documents to be added, the subscription of database and the digitization or conversion of documents to an appropriate digital form.

iii. Indexing and storage

This component carries out the indexing and storage of documents and metadata for efficient search and retrieval.

iv. Search and retrieval

This is the digital library interface used by the end users to browse, search, retrieve and view the contents of the digital library. It is typically presented to the users as Hyper-Text Mark-up Language (HTML) page.

1.7   Aim of Work

The aim of project is to design and implements an E- Library for the students of special University. Digital Libraries basically store materials in electronic format and manipulate large collections of those materials effectively. The e-library system facilitate the process of search and downloads of books as well as offers the ability to select, retrieve and update information.

1.8   Chapters Outlines

Chapter one: Introduction

This chapter gives and introduction to the Electronic library functions and features. After that the objective from the design and implementation of the project is described.

Chapter Two: E-library Concepts

This chapter gives an introduction to E-library concepts and components.

Chapter Three: Design and Implementation

This chapter describes the steps to design the E-library Website in details. After that, the implementation of E-library and user access are described.

Chapter Four: Conclusion & Future Works

This chapter describe the key points concluded from the implementation of the E-library website.

E-library Concepts

2.1 Introduction

This Chapter gives an introduction to E-library concepts and its history. After that needs of E-library system are described in details. Then, PHP programming language and its characteristics are described. Finally, MySQL Database and Apache server are introduced. Finally, Web Architecture and the World Wide Web are described in details.

2.2 Introduction to Digital Library

Digital Libraries are being created today for diverse communities and in different fields e.g. education, science, culture, development, health, governance and so on. With the availability of several free digital Library software packages at the recent time, the creation and sharing of information through the digital library collections has become an attractive and feasible proposition for library and information professionals around the world. Library automation has helped to provide easy access to collections through the use of computerized library catalogue such as On-line Public Access Catalog (OPAC) [6].

Digital libraries differ significantly from the traditional libraries because they allow users to gain an on-line access to and work with the electronic versions of full text documents and their associated images. Many digital libraries also provide an access to other multi-media content like audio and video. A digital library is a

9

collection of digital documents or objects. This definition is the dominant perception of many people of today. Nevertheless, Smith (2001) defined a digital library as an organized and focused collection of digital objects, including text, images, video and audio, with the methods of access and retrieval and for the selection, creation, organization, maintenance and sharing of collection. Though the focus of this definition is on the document collection, it stresses the fact that the digital libraries are much more than a random assembly of digital objects. They retain the several qualities of traditional libraries such as a defined community of users, focused collections, long-term availability, and the possibility of selecting, organizing, preserving and sharing resources [6].

The digital libraries are sometimes perceived as institutions, though this is not as dominant as the previous definition. The following definition given by the Digital Library Federation (DLF) brings out the essence of this perception. Digital Libraries are organization that provide the resources, including the specialized staff to select, structure, offer intellectual access to interpret, distribute, preserve the integrity of and ensure the persistence over time of collections of digital works so that they are readily and economically available for use by a defined community or set of communities." (DLF 2001) [6].

2.3 Needs for E-library

Need for a digital librarian in the management of digital information system Necessity is the mother of invention. The emerging global digital libraries or world-wide digital information centers generate the need for creating a new job-title ``digital librarian'' to manage their digital knowledge resources. The huge digital libraries are emerging as knowledge warehouses. Digital librarians are required to [7]:

- Manage the digital libraries;
- Organize digital knowledge and information;
- disseminate digital information from the computer-held digital information;
- provide digital reference services and electronic information services;
- provide knowledge mining from the
- emerging knowledge warehouses;
- handle the tasks of massive digitization, digital storage process, and digital preservation;
- provide universal access and retrieval of digital knowledge, ultimately access to all;
- Catalogue and classify digital documents and digital knowledge.

2.4 History of Internet

During the past thirty years digital libraries have gone from a curiosity to mainstream. The 1990s were a particularly formative decade. Before 1990 computing in libraries had concentrated on metadata. MARC cataloguing had reached its zenith, indexing services such as Medline had developed sophisticated search languages, and Science Citation Index was the state-of-art in linked data, but with very few exceptions the actual collections were physical items such as printed documents. About 1990, computing reached a level where it became economically possible to mount large collections online and to access them over networks. The result was a flurry of experiments and prototypes. Many are almost forgotten, yet the libraries of today were formed by the energy and creativity of these efforts. This article describes some of these projects and the impact that they have had on modern libraries [7]

11

There was nothing inevitable about which prototypes succeeded in the long term. The Internet uses the TCP/IP family of protocols, but for many years the Open Systems Interconnection (OSI) framework was the choice of every major company. The early web was one of several competing ways to mount information online and had many weaknesses. Web searching did not have to be a free service paid for by advertising. Engineers might argue that the successful technology was technically superior, but cultural, economic, and social forces were at least as important in its adoption [7].

2.5 Web Browsers

A Web browser is a program that displays Web pages and other documents on the Web. Unfortunately, different browsers may interpret the HTML of Web pages somewhat differently, and thus, when you create Web pages remember that they may appear different when viewed in various browsers. The University supports the browsers illustrated below, which can be downloaded free from the company's Web site. A browser has the ability to get a web page from a web server somewhere, interpret the HTML code, fetch the referenced files, and then construct the page on your computer monitor to look as the designer intended [8].

2.6 The basic functions of a web browser

Web browsers can run on most operating systems with limited hardware or software requirement. They are the graphic user interface for the clients to interact with web applications. The basic functions of a web browser include [9]:

- Interpret HTML markup and present documents visually.

12

- Support hyperlinks in HTML documents so the clicking on such a hyperlink can lead to the corresponding HTML file being downloaded from the same or another web server and presented.

- Use HTML form and the HTTP protocol to send requests and data to web applications and download HTML documents.

- Maintain cookies (name value pairs, explained later) deposited on client computers by a web application and send all cookies back to a web site if they are deposited by the web application at that web site (cookies will be further discussed later in this chapter).

- Use plug-in applications to support extra functions like playing audio-video files and running Java applets.

- Implement a *web browser sandbox* security policy: any software component (applets, JavaScripts, ActiveX,..etc) running inside a web browser normally cannot access local clients' resources like files or keyboards, and can only communicate directly with applications on the web server from where it is downloaded [9].

The web server is mainly for receiving document requests and data submission from web browsers through the HTTP protocol on top of the Internet's TCP/IP layer. The main function of the web server is to feed HTML files to the web browsers. If the client is requesting a static existing file, it will be retrieved on a server hard disk and sent back to the web browser right away. If the client needs customized HTML pages like the client's bank statement, a software component, like a JSP page or a servlet class (the "Extension" box in the web architecture figure), needs to retrieve the client's data from the database and compose a response HTML file on-the-fly [9].

2.7 Uniform Resource Locators (URL)

A web server program runs multiple web applications (sites) hosted in different folders under the web server program's document root folder. A server computer may run multiple server programs including web servers. Each server program on a server computer uses a port number, between 0 and 65535, unique on the server machine as its local identification (by default a web server uses port 80). Each server computer has an IP address, like 198.105.44.27, as its unique identifier on the Internet. Domain names, like www.pace.edu, are used as user-friendly identifications of server computers, and they are mapped to IP addresses by a Domain Name Server (DNS). A Uniform Resource Locator (URL) is an address for uniquely identifying a web resource (like a web page or a Java object) on the Internet, and it has the following general format:

http://domain-name:port/application/resource?query-string

standing for *secure HTTP* and *File Transfer Protocol*); *application* is a server-side folder containing all resources related to a web application; *resource* could be the name (alias or nickname) of an HTML or script/program file residing on a server hard disk; and the optional query string passes user data to the web server. An example URL is http://www.amazon.com/computer/sale?model=dell610.

There is a special domain name "localhost" that is normally defined as an alias of local IP address 127.0.0.1. Domain name "localhost" and IP address 127.0.0.1 are for addressing a local computer, very useful for testing web applications where the web browser and the web server are running on the same computer.

Most computers are on the Internet as well as on a local area network (LAN), like home wireless network, and they have an external IP address and a local IP address. To find out what is your computer's external IP address on the Internet, use a web browser to visit http://whatismyip.com. To find out what is your local (home) IP address, on Windows, run "ipconfig" in a DOS window; and on Linux, run "sudoifconfig" in a terminal window [9].

2.8 World Wide Web (WWW)

The Web represents the application of hypertext technology and a graphical interface to the Internet to retrieve information that is contained in specially funneled documents that may reside in the same computer or be distributed across many computers around the world. It consists of three main elements. The Hypertext Markup Language (HTML) comprises the programming codes, or tags, that define fonts, layouts, embedge5i graphics, and links (hyperlinks) to other documents accessible via the Web. The Hypertext Transfer Protocol (HTTP) defines a set of standards for transmitting Web pages across the Internet [10].

The Universal Resource Locator (URL) is a standardized naming convention for identifying a Web document or file, in a sense the address of a link. The result is called the Web because it is made up of many sites, all linked together, with users traveling from one site to the next by clicking a computer's pointing device on a hyperlink [8]. The World Wide Web provide a system of interlinked, hypertext documents that runs over the Internet With a Web browser, a user views Web pages that exchange text, graphics, and other multimedia and navigates between them using hyperlinks [10].

2.9 Introduction to Pre-Hypertext Programming (PHP) Language

PHP is one of the most popular languages used on the internet. It is a computer scripting language, originally designed for producing dynamic web pages. It is for server-side scripting. PHP is excellent for creating dynamic Web sites based on

15

database content or different characteristics of browsers. The most common delimiters are *"<? php"* and *"?>"*, which are open and close delimiters respectively [11].

2.9.1. Characteristics of PHP

As you may have realized, the PHP language revolves around the central theme of practicality. PHP is about providing the programmer with the necessary tools to get the job done in a quick and efficient fashion. Five important characteristics make PHP's practical nature possible [11]:

- **Simplicity**

A PHP script can consist of 10,000 lines or one line: whatever you need to get the job done. There is no need to include libraries, special compilation directives, or anything of the sort. The PHP engine simply begins executing the code after the first escape sequence (<?) and continues until it passes the closing escape sequence (?>). If the code is syntactically correct, it will be executed exactly as it is displayed.

- **Familiarity**

Programmers from many backgrounds will find themselves already accustomed to the PHP language. Many of the language's constructs are borrowed from C and Perl, and in many cases PHP code is almost indistinguishable from that found in the typical C or Pascal program. This minimizes the learning curve considerably.

- **Efficiency**

Efficiency is an extremely important consideration for working in a multiuser environment such as the WWW. PHP 4.0 introduced resource allocation mechanisms and more pronounced support for object-oriented programming, in

16

addition to session management features. Reference counting has also been introduced in the latest version, eliminating unnecessary memory allocation.

- **Security**

PHP provides developers and administrators with a flexible and efficient set of security safeguards. These safeguards can be divided into two frames of reference: system level and application level.

- **Flexibility**

Because PHP is an embedded language, it is extremely flexible towards meeting the needs of the developer. Although PHP is generally touted as being used in conjunction solely with HTML, it can also be integrated alongside languages like JavaScript, WML, XML, and many others. Additionally, as with most other mainstream languages, wisely planned PHP applications can be easily expanded as needed.

Finally, PHP offers access to external components, such as Enterprise Java Beans and Win32 COM objects. These newly added features put PHP in the big league, truly enabling developers to scale PHP projects upward and outward as need be.

- **Free**

The open source development strategy has gained considerable notoriety in the software industry. The prospect of releasing source code to the masses has resulted in undeniably positive outcomes for many projects, perhaps most notably Linux, although the success of the Apache project has certainly been a major contributor in proving the validity of the open source ideal. The same holds true for the developmental history of PHP, as users worldwide have been a huge factor in the advancement of the PHP project.

2.10 Introduction to MYSQL Database.

MySQL is a relational database server that supports the well-known SQL (Structured Query Language) database language. Therefore, MySQL is named after the language that developers use to store, query, and later update data in a MySQL database. In short, SQL is the native language of MySQL. MySQL can store many types of data from something as tiny as a single character to as large as complete files or graphics. Although it can be accessed by most programming languages, it is often coupled with PHP because they work together with case. Information stored in a MySQL database hosted on a web server can be accessed from anywhere in the world with a computer. This makes it a good way to store information that needs [12].

Chapter three

The Proposed Electronic Library Of University

The design of **Electronic Library for the university** consists of many phases each phase have an algorithm for it design also there are many tools used to implement the design of web site and the **electronic library**.

3.1 Hardware and Software Requirements

To implement the design of E-library system, the following set of hardware and software requirements used:

1.Hardware requirements are divided into:
a.Client: is a machine used to access and use the designed smart of E-library system through a web interface.
b.Server: which is a machine used to host the proposed smart of E-library system database and website, WAMP server is installed on the server node as a database and web server to offer services to clients.(Wamp server): Wamp Server is a Windows web development environment. It allows you to create web applications with Apache2, PHP and a MySQL database. Alongside, PhpMyAdmin allows you to manage easily your databases[6].

3.2 Software and Programming Languages Used

a. Hypertext Mark-up Language (HTML): HTML is the authoring language used to create documents on the World Wide Web[7].

b. JavaScript: JavaScript is a language commonly used in web development. It was originally developed by Netscape as a means to add dynamic and interactive elements to websites.

c. Hypertext Pre-processor (PHP) Language: PHP is a script language and interpreter that is freely available and used primarily on Linux Web servers. PHP, originally derived from Personal Home Page Tools, now stands for PHP: Hypertext Preprocessor, which the PHP FAQ describes as a "recursive acronym."

d. MySQL Database is a relational database server that supports the well-known SQL (Structured Query Language) database language. Therefore, MySQL is named after the language that developers use to store, query, and later update data in a MySQL database. In short, SQL is the native language of MySQL. MySQL can store many types of data from something as tiny as a single character to as large as complete files or graphics. Although it can be accessed by most programming languages, it is often coupled with PHP because they work together with case. Information stored in a MySQL database hosted on a web server can be accessed from anywhere in the world with a computer. This makes it a good way to store information that needs [7].

3.3 The security of system

To keeping that system secure. there are some tips concerned about the security of Apache server:

- **Enable ModSecurity**: ModSecurity is a free Web Application Firewall that works with Apache. It uses a flexible rule engine to perform simple and complex operations to prevent attacks like SQL injection, cross-site scripting, Trojans, bad user agents, session hijacking, and much more. By default, ModSecurity isn't installed. To install ModSecurity, follow these steps.
- Open a terminal window on your Apache server.
- Issue the command sudo apt-get install libapache2-modsecurity.
- Rename the sample config file with the command sudo mv /etc/modsecurity/modsecurity.conf-recommended /etc/modsecurity/modsecurity.conf.
- Open the newly created file for editing with the command sudo nano /etc/modsecurity/modsecurity.conf.
- Add the line SecRuleEngine On in the Rule engine initialization section.
- Restart Apache with the command sudo service apache2 restart.
  to edit the ModSecurity configuration file. Open that file with the command sudo nano /etc/apache2/mods-enabled/security2.conf and add the following lines:

IncludeOptional "/usr/share/modsecurity-crs/*.conf"
IncludeOptional "/usr/share/modsecurity-crs/base_rules/*.conf

Save and close that file and restart Apache with the command sudo service apache2 restart.

- **Limit large requests By default**, Apache does not set a limit to the size of HTTP requests it will accept; this can lead to an attacker sending a lot of data to take down the server. This is configured on a per-directory basis.
- **Restrict browsing to specific directories** the users to don't be able to browse outside of specific directories.

3.4 Design Phases

The design consist of two main phases and many others sub-phases

1. The First Main Phase (The Administrator Side)
the administrator login page of the designed E-library website. It contains two fields the username and password. If the administrator enter correct information, the system will redirect the administrator to Admin home page, otherwise the shows a message that the username or password error. The administrator have many responsibilities to do such as check the user that want to register in the electronic library (checking algorithm) ,add, delete new book or thesis, Reports Page and Resource books Report page.

3.4.1 Checking(Authentication) Algorithm
Input : The request of registration
Output : approve or disapprove the request of registration
Step 1: Begin
Step 2:the administrator take the information of user that entered in the registration form(name of user, date of birthday and his department in the university)
Step 3: the administrator search the **Central Data Base** about the information of the user to assurance the authorization (the registration department in the university control and continue update the central data base that have the names of all student and members of university)
Step 4:

4.1 if the information of user found in the **Central Database then**

    4.1.1 The administrator search the **Users Database** (the users database control and update by the administrator of the system) about the username and password of the user to avoid the confliction and also to avoid register the same user with more than user name ,**if** the information not found in users data

base **Then**

a. The administrator approve the registration request

b. Add the user name and password and the registration information to the users

   database. **Otherwise**

4.2 The administrator disapprove the registration request

4.2.1 The administrator send a declaration message to the user about reasons of disapproving the registration request.

Step 5:End.

3.4.2 The Administrator Responsibilities

The administrator have many responsibilities to do for manage the electronic library, these responsibilities are begin after the administrator login to page of the designed E-library website. It contains two fields the username and password. If the administrator enter correct information, the system will redirect the administrator to Admin home page, otherwise the shows a message to user that the username or password error, the administrator responsibilities are:

a. Add New (Book, thesis)

the Add books, **thesis's** page of the e-library website allows the administrator of to add information and digital copy of the book to the system ,the information are (Book Title, Library Class, Book Class, Book Author, Edition Number, The Publisher, Number Of Copies, Resource Of Textbox, ISBN, Date Of Insertion, The Type Of File Of Book, The Chosen Department).

b. Delete Books page

The edit books page of the designed e-library website allows the administrator of the website to edit information or the digital copy of the required books. It also allows the administrator to delete books. to delete any book or thesis the administrator must enter the book title and author to search the database of e-books and find it, then all the information about the book will appear the administrator will delete the book and its information, the same process will execute when the administrator want to delete any thesis.

c. Reports Page

The reports page of the administrator phase of E-library website contains the reports about books like resource books report, Books specialty report and textbox report. It also contains report for thesis like Thesis title reports and Supervisor report for example(**Resource books Report page** :It presents report contains book name, author, number of book copies and publish date).

Insert digital documents(books,thesis's) ,retrieve the information, locating, indexing sorting, filtering and searching of the digital documents, archiving, digital document storage ,management of digital information system ,classification of the digital documents	tasks ofthe administrator of e-library

2. The Second Main Phase (The User(Student) Side)

The Users of the E-library can be accessed at any time anywhere over the internet through the designed GUI interfaces using the internet browser by writing the URL of the website. The E-library website can be accessed using various types of client devices such desktop, laptop or mobile devices. then if the user it the first time he visit the website he must be registrations otherwise he must be login to the system ,

24

The main function that the user can perform it was divided into three parts: the user registration, the user login and the user logout of website.

3.5 Algorithms Of User Side

to assurance the authentication of the user of the online e-library the user must perform some actions such as the registration in the website, login and after he visits the website ,he must logout of e-library

3.5.1 Login Algorithm

Input : The username and password
Output : Redirect the user to users home page .
Step 1: Begin
Step 2: If the user enter correct information, the system will redirect the user to users home page (this mean the user was registered in the website previously) And he can perform the operation that specified to him**(user operations algorithm)**
Step 3: otherwise the shows a message to user that the username or password error.**(this mean the user wasn't registered in the website previously)**)the user must first complete the Registration process **(Registration Algorithm)**before login to the system

Step 4:End.

3.5.2 Registration Algorithm

Input : The user information
Output : Complete the user registration process
Step 1: Begin.
Step 2: The user fill the registration field: name, e-mail, password ,date of birthday ,department.

25

Step 3:the user click register button

Step4: After that the registration request is displayed for the administrator.

- **If** the administrator approve student registration(Administration Algorithm),then the student can access to e-library via username and password.

- **Else** message is displayed to the student that this username and password is not registered

Step5:End.

3.5.3 User Operations Algorithm

Input : The user login to the website.
Output : The user **view or download** the books or thesis .
Step 1: Begin
Step 2: The user login to website by enter the correct user name and password in user management Interface
Step 3: if the user select the books page of the e-library website. It views the books archived in e-library with basic information like book name, author, ISBN and publish year This page allows the students to **view** and **download** books and also search for books using book title and author.
else if the user select Thesis page It views the Thesis archived in e-library with basic information like Thesis title, researcher name and supervisor. This page allows the students to **view** and **download** thesis and also search for thesis using thesis title, researcher of supervisor.
Step 4: The user must logout from the website after he finish his work
Step 5:End.

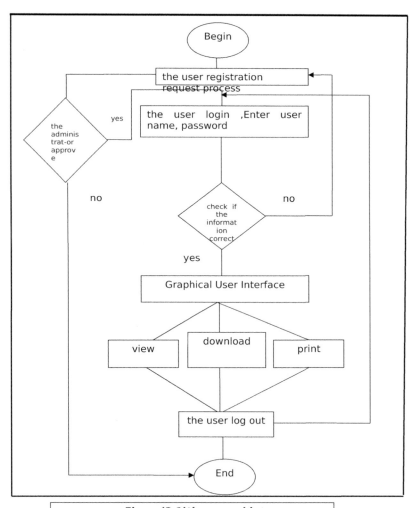

Begin

the user registration request process

the user login ,Enter user name, password

the adminis trat-or approv e

yes

no

check if the informat ion correct

no

yes

Graphical User Interface

view

download

print

the user log out

End

Figure(3-1)the user side

27

3.6 Database Tables Structure

The database of the E-library system is designed and created by using WAMP server and MySQL database. The database contains the following tables:

a. Students Table: contains information about students stored and registered in the databased as shown in figure 3.1.

#	Name	Type	Collation
1	id	int(10)	
2	name	varchar(100)	utf8_unicode_ci
3	u_name	varchar(100)	utf8_unicode_ci
4	pass	text	utf8_unicode_ci
5	d_birth	date	
6	dept	varchar(30)	utf8_unicode_ci
7	status	int(1)	

Figure 3.1 Students Table.

b. Books Table: contains information about books that stored in the database.

#	Name	Type	Collation
1	id	int(10)	
2	b_title	varchar(100)	utf8_unicode_ci
3	b_author	varchar(100)	utf8_unicode_ci
4	lib_class	varchar(100)	utf8_unicode_ci
5	b_class	varchar(100)	utf8_unicode_ci
6	isbn	varchar(30)	utf8_unicode_ci
7	b_desc	varchar(1000)	utf8_unicode_ci
8	b_rack	varchar(20)	utf8_unicode_ci
9	edition_no	varchar(30)	utf8_unicode_ci
10	edition_year	date	
11	publisher	varchar(100)	utf8_unicode_ci
12	copyright	varchar(100)	utf8_unicode_ci
13	no_copy	int(4)	
14	b_type	varchar(100)	utf8_unicode_ci
15	type	varchar(100)	utf8_unicode_ci
16	status	int(1)	

Figure 3.2 Books Table Structure.

c.Thesis Table: contains information about thesis that stored in the database.

#	Name	Type	Collation
1	id	int(10)	
2	title	varchar(100)	utf8_unicode_ci
3	researcher	varchar(100)	utf8_unicode_ci
4	supervisor	varchar(100)	utf8_unicode_ci
5	thesis_no	varchar(30)	utf8_unicode_ci
6	thesis_year	date	
7	study_type	varchar(100)	utf8_unicode_ci
8	issuer	varchar(100)	utf8_unicode_ci
9	specialization	varchar(100)	utf8_unicode_ci
10	status	int(1)	

Figure 3.3 Thesis Structure Table.

29

d.Download table: contains information of books and thesis downloaded ae well as information of students.

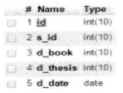

Figure 3.4 Download Table Structure.

3.6.1 Hardware and Software Requirements

To design and implement the E-library system, the following set of hardware and software requirements used:

Hardware requirements are divided into:

c.Client: is a machine used to access and use the designed smart of E-library system through a web interface.

d.Server: which is a machine used to host the proposed smart of E-library system database and website, WAMP server is installed on the server node as a database and webserver to offer services to clients.

e.WAMP Server: Wamp Server is a Windows web development environment. It allows you to create web applications with Apache2, PHP and a MySQL database. Alongside, PhpMyAdmin allows you to manage easily the databases

3.7 E-library Implementation

The implementation of the designed E-library system includes the following phases:

3.7.1vSoftware and Programming Languages Used

e. Hypertext Markup Language (HTML): HTML is the authoring language used to create documents on the World Wide Web. HTML is similar to SGML, although it is not a strict subset.

f. JavaScript: JavaScript is a programming language commonly used in web development. It was originally developed by Netscape as a means to add dynamic and interactive elements to websites. While JavaScript is influenced by Java, the syntax is more similar to C and is based on ECMAScript, a scripting language developed by Sun Microsystems.

g. Hypertext Preprocessor (PHP) Language: PHP is a script language and interpreter that is freely available and used primarily on Linux Web servers. PHP, originally derived from Personal Home Page Tools, now stands for PHP: Hypertext Preprocessor, which the PHP FAQ describes as a "recursive acronym."

h. MySQL Database (Wamp server): Wamp Server is a Windows web development environment. It allows you to create web applications with Apache2, PHP and a MySQL database. Alongside, PhpMyAdmin allows you to manage easily your databases.

- **The E-library Access**

The Users of the E-library system can be accessed at any time anywhere over the internet through the designed GUI interfaces using the internet browser by writing the URL of the website. The E-library website can be accessed using various types of client devices such desktop, laptop or mobile devices.

3.7.2 E-library Phases and Services

a. Students Registration and Login Page

Figure 3.5 and 3.6 shows the login page of E-library website. It contains two fields the username and password. If the user enter correct information, the system will redirect the user to users home page, otherwise the shows a message to user that the username or password error.

Figure 3-5 Students Login Page.

Figure 3.6 shows the registration phase of E-library. The student cannot signing to the library till he register in the system. The student fill the registration field and click register button. After that the registration request is displayed in user management phase of administrator. If the administrator approve student registration, then the student can access to e-library via username and password, else message is displayed to the student that this username and password is not registered as shown in figure 3.7.

Figure 3.6 Student registration page.

Figure 3.7 user management Interface.

b. **Books Page**

Figure 3.8 shows the books page of the e-library website. It views the books archived in e-library with basic information like book name, author, ISBN and publish year. This page allows the students to download books and also search for books using book title and author.

Figure 3.8 Books Page.

c. Thesis Page

Figure 3.9 shows the Thesis page of the designed website. It views the Thesis archived in e-library with basic information like Thesis title, researcher name and supervisor. This page allows the students to view and borrow thesis and also search for thesis using thesis title, researcher of supervisor.

35

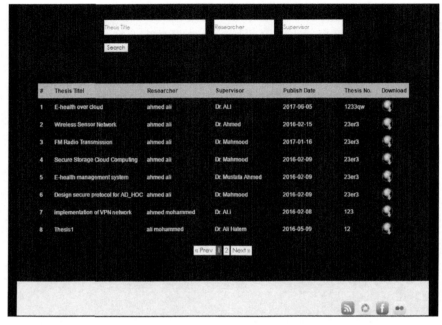

Figure 3.9 Thesis Page.

d. Administrator Login Page

Figure 3.10 shows the administrator login page of the designed E-library website. It contains two fields the username and password. If the administrator enter correct information, the system will redirect the administrator to Admin home page, otherwise the shows a message to user that the username or password error.

Figure 3.10 Administrator Login Page.

e. Add New Book

Figure 3.11 shows the Add books page of the e-library website. It allows the administrator of the website to add information and digital copy of the book to the system to view to student's book page shown in figure 3.7.

37

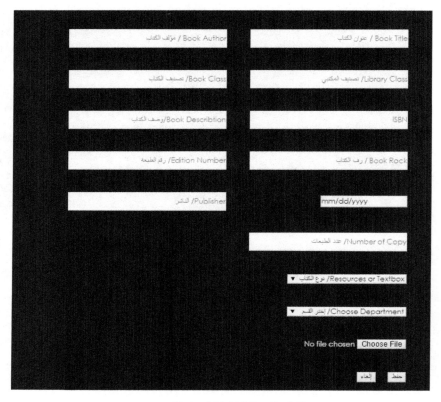

Figure 3.11 Add New Book Page.

f. Delete Books page

Figure 3.12 shows edit books page of the designed e-library website. It allows the administrator of the website to edit information or the digital copy of the required books. It also allows the administrator to delete books.

38

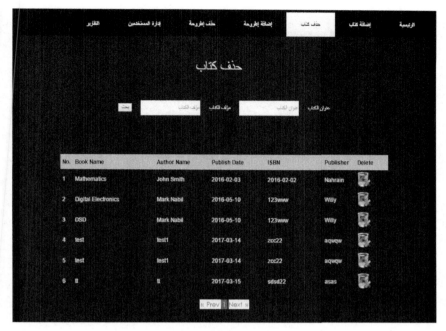

Figure 3.12 Delete Books Page.

g. Reports Page

Figure 3.13 shows the reports page of the administrator phase of E-library website. It contains reports about books like resource books report, Books specialty report and textbox report. It also contains report for thesis like Thesis title reports and Supervisor report.

39

Figure 3.13 Reports Page.

Figure 3.14 Resource books report page.

h. Resource books Report page

Figure 3.14 shows the resource books report page of the designed E-library website in the administrator phase. It presents report contains book name, author, number of book copies and publish date.

Conclusions

4.1 Conclusion

With the development of science and technology ,The E-library plays an important role in education sector these days. Its success depends upon the sharing of useful information and documentation of it. The Electronic libraries can provide a vehicle for extending collaboration, which is at the heart of the academy, with the aim of more effective education. The Digital Libraries basically store materials in electronic format and the administrator can use an E-library management system to add, modify or delete the objects from the database by using online control that is protected with a username and password and e-mail for more authentication also The e-library system facilitates of different departments in the same universities to access , search and download the required books and thesis's.

References

1. https://en.wikipedia.org/wiki/website.

2. https://www.pinterest.com/pin/450148925229630402

3. https://www.linkedin.com/pulse/website-development-master-systems-pvt-ltd-apr 3, 2017

4. http://www.imaxq.com/article.php?article=3&name=website-design-and-development-with-history

5. prof. lixin tao, introduction to web technologies, pace university, http://csis.pace.edu/ulixin.

6. Ibrahim Usman Alhaji, "Digitization of Library Resources and the formation of digital libraries: A practical approach ".

7. V. Sreenivasulu, "The role of a digital librarian in the management of digital information systems (DIS)" 2000.

8. "Web design 1: Introduction to creating a website using Dreamweaver MX Practical workbook", University of Bristol, 2005.

9. Li-Chiou Chen & Lixin Tao, "Introduction to Web Technologies", Pace University, 2011

10. Tony Johnson, "Spinning the World Wide Web" 1994.

11. Robin Nixon, "A step by step guide to dynamic websites: Learning PHP, MySQL and JavaScript", 2009.

12. C. A. Bell, "Expert MySQL" Apress, USA, 2007.

13. V.Franklin David Jebaraj, M.Deivasigamani "The Electronic Library : An Indian Scenario",Library Philosophy and Practice Vol. 5, No. 2 (Spring 2003)

14. K. Calhoun, Social Roles of Digital Libraries, Exploring Digital Libraries: Foundations, Practice, Prospects. London : Facet Publishing, 2014.

15. F. Wangila. "An Assessment of the Implementation of Digital Library Technologies in Institutions of Higher Learning: A Case Study of Kenyatta University", International Journal of Academic Research in Business and Social Sciences, vol. 4, 532-541, 2014

16. T.C. Huang, "What Library 2.0 has taught libraries in Taiwan about e-learning", The Electronic Library, vol. 33, pp. 1121-1132, 2015 .

17. Digital libraries in education. Moscow: UNESCO Institute for Information Technologies in Education, 2003. Retrieved October 22, 2016. from http://iite.unesco.org/pics/publications/en/files/3214609.pdf

18. V. Sreenivasulu. "The role of a digital librarian in the management of digital information systems (DIS)", The Electronic Library, vol. 18, pp. 12-20, 2000.

Printed in Great Britain
by Amazon

85400645R00037